Closer than Ever

A back and forth journal for couples

by Emma Grace Harper

Her Info:

Name: _____

Current age: _____

Age when we started dating: _____

Our anniversary date: _____

Date we started this journal: _____

⋈⋈⋈⋈⋈⋈⋈⋈⋈⋈

His Info:

Name: _____

Current age: _____

Age when we started dating: _____

How long we have been together: _____

Date we finished this journal: _____

How this journal works

She fills out this page as if her partner asked her the prompt, then passes the journal to him.

He writes his response below her answer & then on the next page answers the prompt as if she asked the question, then hands the journal back to her.

Keep the exchange going and enjoy!

PS: Whenever you feel like there is more to say than what you can write down, take time with your partner to talk about the questions and go as deep as you like! :)

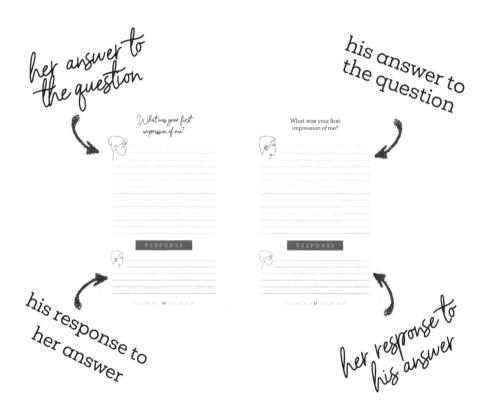

her answer to the question

his answer to the question

his response to her answer

her response to his answer

Fun and Creative Ways to Make Your Couples Journal Exchange Extra Special

Hide and Seek: After filling out a prompt, hide the journal somewhere for your partner to find, like under their pillow or in a drawer, as a surprise.

Date Night Exchange: Make it a tradition to exchange the journal during date nights and share your answers over dinner or a cozy night in.

Travel Companion: Bring it along on trips and fill out a few pages in new places to capture memories of your adventures together.

Weekend Ritual: Dedicate a time each weekend to sit down together, fill out a page, and reflect on each other's answers.

Random Acts of Love: Leave the journal open to a completed page with a heartfelt answer for your partner to read when they need a little pick-me-up.

Reflection Anniversary: Every few months, look back on what you both wrote to see how your perspectives or feelings have grown.

Add Small Surprises: Occasionally slip in little notes, tickets from a memorable event, or photos to make it even more special.

TABLE OF CONTENTS

"Love is not just about finding the right person, but creating the right relationship.
It's about knowing and understanding each other better every day."

- Anonymous -

Getting to know
each other better

What is your favorite childhood memory?

_____
_____
_____
_____
_____
_____
_____
_____
_____
_____
_____
_____
_____
_____

RESPONSE

_____
_____
_____
_____
_____

What is your favorite childhood memory?

What was your first impression of me?

What was your first impression of me?

_____

_____

_____

_____

_____

_____

_____

_____

_____

_____

_____

_____

_____

RESPONSE

_____

_____

_____

_____

_____

What's your happiest memory from when we first started dating?

_____
_____
_____
_____
_____
_____
_____
_____
_____
_____
_____
_____

RESPONSE

_____
_____
_____
_____
_____

What's your happiest memory from when we first started dating?

_____

_____

_____

_____

_____

_____

_____

_____

_____

_____

_____

_____

_____

_____

_____

RESPONSE

_____

_____

_____

_____

_____

_____

How did you know you wanted to be with me?

_____
_____
_____
_____
_____
_____
_____
_____
_____
_____
_____
_____

RESPONSE

_____
_____
_____
_____
_____

How did you know you wanted to be with me?

RESPONSE

What's a small thing I do that makes your day better?

_____
_____
_____
_____
_____
_____
_____
_____
_____
_____
_____
_____
_____

RESPONSE

_____
_____
_____
_____
_____
_____

What's a small thing I do that makes your day better?

_____
_____
_____
_____
_____
_____
_____
_____
_____
_____
_____
_____
_____

RESPONSE

_____
_____
_____
_____
_____

What's the most important lesson you've learned in life?

_____
_____
_____
_____
_____
_____
_____
_____
_____
_____
_____
_____
_____
_____
_____

RESPONSE

_____
_____
_____
_____
_____
_____

What's the most important lesson you've learned in life?

_____
_____
_____
_____
_____
_____
_____
_____
_____
_____
_____
_____
_____
_____

RESPONSE

_____
_____
_____
_____
_____
_____

What's one thing you admire about me that you've never told me?

_____
_____
_____
_____
_____
_____
_____
_____
_____
_____
_____
_____
_____
_____
_____

_____
_____
_____
_____
_____

What's one thing you admire about me that you've never told me?

_____

_____

_____

_____

_____

_____

_____

_____

_____

_____

_____

_____

_____

_____

_____

RESPONSE

_____

_____

_____

_____

_____

_____

What's your favorite thing we do together?

_____
_____
_____
_____
_____
_____
_____
_____
_____
_____
_____
_____
_____

RESPONSE

_____
_____
_____
_____
_____
_____

What's your favorite thing we do together?

_____

_____

_____

_____

_____

_____

_____

_____

_____

_____

_____

_____

_____

_____

_____

RESPONSE

_____

_____

_____

_____

_____

"Sometimes, looking back
on our journey together
is the best way to see how
far we've come."

- Anonymous -

CHAPTER 2

Reflecting on our
relationship

What's the biggest challenge we've overcome as a couple?

_____
_____
_____
_____
_____
_____
_____
_____
_____
_____
_____
_____
_____

RESPONSE

_____
_____
_____
_____

What's the biggest challenge we've overcome as a couple?

_____
_____
_____
_____
_____
_____
_____
_____
_____
_____
_____
_____
_____

RESPONSE

_____
_____
_____
_____
_____
_____

What's a goal we've achieved together that you're proud of?

_____
_____
_____

_____
_____
_____
_____
_____
_____
_____
_____
_____
_____

RESPONSE

_____
_____
_____
_____
_____

What's a goal we've achieved together that you're proud of?

RESPONSE

How do you feel we've grown since we first met?

_____
_____
_____
_____
_____
_____
_____
_____
_____
_____
_____
_____
_____

RESPONSE

_____
_____
_____
_____
_____
_____

How do you feel we've grown since we first met?

_____

_____

_____

_____

_____

_____

_____

_____

_____

_____

_____

_____

_____

_____

_____

RESPONSE

_____

_____

_____

_____

_____

_____

What's the most romantic thing we've done together?

RESPONSE

What's the most romantic thing we've done together?

RESPONSE

What's one thing we could do to strengthen our relationship even more?

_____
_____
_____
_____
_____
_____
_____
_____
_____
_____
_____
_____
_____

RESPONSE

_____
_____
_____
_____
_____
_____

What's one thing we could do to strengthen our relationship even more?

_____

_____

_____

_____

_____

_____

_____

_____

_____

_____

_____

_____

RESPONSE

_____

_____

_____

_____

_____

When do you feel closest to me?

_____
_____
_____
_____
_____
_____
_____
_____
_____
_____
_____
_____
_____

RESPONSE

_____
_____
_____
_____
_____
_____

When do you feel closest
to me?

_____

_____

_____

_____

_____

_____

_____

_____

_____

_____

_____

_____

_____

_____

RESPONSE

_____

_____

_____

_____

_____

How do you like to express love in our relationship?

_____
_____
_____
_____
_____
_____
_____
_____
_____
_____
_____
_____
_____

RESPONSE

_____
_____
_____
_____
_____
_____

How do you like to express love in our relationship?

What are some of the things you value most about our relationship?

_____
_____
_____
_____
_____
_____
_____
_____
_____
_____
_____
_____
_____
_____

_____
_____
_____
_____
_____
_____

What are some of the things you value most about our relationship?

_____

_____

_____

_____

_____

_____

_____

_____

_____

_____

_____

_____

_____

RESPONSE

_____

_____

_____

_____

_____

_____

"A dream you dream
alone is only a dream.
A dream you dream
together is reality."

- John Lennon -

CHAPTER 3

Our hopes and
dreams

What's one thing you hope we'll experience together in the future?

_____
_____
_____
_____
_____
_____
_____
_____
_____
_____
_____
_____
_____

RESPONSE

_____
_____
_____
_____
_____

What's one thing you hope we'll experience together in the future?

_____

_____

_____

_____

_____

_____

_____

_____

_____

_____

_____

_____

_____

_____

RESPONSE

_____

_____

_____

_____

_____

_____

How do you imagine our life in 10 years?

_____
_____
_____
_____
_____
_____
_____
_____
_____
_____
_____
_____
_____

RESPONSE

_____
_____
_____
_____
_____

How do you imagine our life in 10 years?

_____

_____

_____

_____

_____

_____

_____

_____

_____

_____

_____

_____

_____

_____

_____

RESPONSE

_____

_____

_____

_____

_____

_____

What's your biggest dream for us as a couple?

_____
_____
_____
_____
_____
_____
_____
_____
_____
_____
_____
_____
_____

RESPONSE

_____
_____
_____
_____
_____
_____

What's your biggest dream for us as a couple?

_____
_____
_____
_____
_____
_____
_____
_____
_____
_____
_____
_____
_____

RESPONSE

_____
_____
_____
_____
_____

If we could live anywhere in the world, where would it be and why?

_____
_____
_____
_____
_____
_____
_____
_____
_____
_____
_____
_____
_____
_____

RESPONSE

_____
_____
_____
_____
_____
_____

If we could live anywhere in the world, where would it be and why?

_____

_____

_____

_____

_____

_____

_____

_____

_____

_____

_____

_____

RESPONSE

_____

_____

_____

_____

_____

What's something new you'd like to learn together?

_____
_____
_____
_____
_____
_____
_____
_____
_____
_____
_____
_____
_____

RESPONSE

_____
_____
_____
_____
_____
_____

What's something new you'd like to learn together?

RESPONSE

What's a tradition you'd love for us to start?

_____
_____
_____
_____
_____
_____
_____
_____
_____
_____
_____
_____

RESPONSE

_____
_____
_____
_____
_____

What's a tradition you'd love for us to start?

RESPONSE

What's one thing you're excited about in our future?

_____

_____

_____

_____

_____

_____

_____

_____

_____

_____

_____

_____

_____

_____

RESPONSE

_____

_____

_____

_____

_____

_____

What's one thing you're excited about in our future?

_____
_____
_____
_____
_____
_____
_____
_____
_____
_____
_____
_____
_____
_____

RESPONSE

_____
_____
_____
_____
_____

What's one thing we could start doing now to make our future even better?

_____
_____
_____
_____
_____
_____
_____
_____
_____
_____
_____
_____
_____

RESPONSE

_____
_____
_____
_____
_____

What's one thing we could start doing now to make our future even better?

_____
_____
_____
_____
_____
_____
_____
_____
_____
_____
_____
_____
_____
_____

RESPONSE

_____
_____
_____
_____
_____
_____

"The deepest love is the one that allows you to become your best self, while sharing your most vulnerable side."

- Anonymous -

CHAPTER 4

Deepening emotional
connection

What's one thing I could do to make you feel more loved?

_____
_____
_____
_____
_____
_____
_____
_____
_____
_____
_____
_____
_____

RESPONSE

_____
_____
_____
_____
_____

What's one thing I could do to make you feel more loved?

RESPONSE

How do you prefer to receive love and affection?

_____
_____
_____
_____
_____
_____
_____
_____
_____
_____
_____
_____
_____
_____

RESPONSE

_____
_____
_____
_____
_____
_____

How do you prefer to receive love and affection?

What's something that makes you feel most appreciated in our relationship?

_____
_____
_____
_____
_____
_____
_____
_____
_____
_____
_____

RESPONSE

_____
_____
_____
_____
_____
_____

What's something that makes you feel most appreciated in our relationship?

_____
_____
_____
_____
_____
_____
_____
_____
_____
_____
_____
_____
_____

RESPONSE

_____
_____
_____
_____
_____
_____

When have you felt most understood by me?

_____
_____
_____
_____
_____
_____
_____
_____
_____
_____
_____
_____
_____
_____

RESPONSE

_____
_____
_____
_____
_____
_____

When have you felt most understood by me?

_____

_____

_____

_____

_____

_____

_____

_____

_____

_____

_____

_____

_____

RESPONSE

_____

_____

_____

_____

_____

What's a vulnerability you've shared with me that made you feel closer to me?

_____
_____
_____
_____
_____
_____
_____
_____
_____
_____
_____
_____
_____

RESPONSE

_____
_____
_____
_____
_____
_____

What's a vulnerability you've shared with me that made you feel closer to me?

How can we better support each other during tough times?

How can we better support each other during tough times?

_____
_____
_____
_____
_____
_____
_____
_____
_____
_____
_____
_____
_____
_____

RESPONSE

_____
_____
_____
_____
_____

What's something that helps you open up more in our conversations?

_____
_____
_____
_____
_____
_____
_____
_____
_____
_____
_____
_____
_____

RESPONSE

_____
_____
_____
_____
_____
_____

What's something that helps you open up more in our conversations?

_____
_____
_____
_____
_____
_____
_____
_____
_____
_____
_____
_____
_____
_____
_____
_____

RESPONSE

_____
_____
_____
_____
_____

What's a fear or insecurity you'd like to talk more openly about?

_____
_____
_____
_____
_____
_____
_____
_____
_____
_____
_____
_____
_____
_____

RESPONSE

_____
_____
_____
_____
_____

What's a fear or insecurity you'd like to talk more openly about?

RESPONSE

"Laughter is an instant vacation."

– Milton Berle –

Laughing together

If we were in a movie, what would our story be about?

_____
_____
_____

_____
_____
_____
_____
_____
_____
_____
_____
_____
_____

RESPONSE

_____
_____
_____
_____
_____

If we were in a movie, what would our story be about?

What's your idea of the perfect date night?

_____
_____
_____
_____
_____
_____
_____
_____
_____
_____
_____
_____
_____

RESPONSE

_____
_____
_____
_____
_____

What's your idea of the perfect date night?

RESPONSE

What's a fun hobby you think we could do together?

_____
_____
_____

_____
_____
_____
_____
_____
_____
_____
_____
_____
_____

RESPONSE

_____
_____
_____
_____
_____

What's a fun hobby you think we could do together?

_____
_____
_____
_____
_____
_____
_____
_____
_____
_____
_____
_____
_____

RESPONSE

_____
_____
_____
_____
_____

What's one thing I do that always makes you laugh?

_____

_____

_____

_____

_____

_____

_____

_____

_____

_____

_____

_____

RESPONSE

_____

_____

_____

_____

_____

What's one thing I do that always makes you laugh?

RESPONSE

What's your favorite way to spend a weekend together?

What's your favorite way to spend a weekend together?

RESPONSE

What's a funny memory we share that you still think about?

_____
_____
_____
_____
_____
_____
_____
_____
_____
_____
_____
_____
_____

RESPONSE

_____
_____
_____
_____
_____

What's a funny memory we share that you still think about?

_____

_____

_____

_____

_____

_____

_____

_____

_____

_____

_____

_____

_____

_____

RESPONSE

_____

_____

_____

_____

_____

If you could plan a surprise day for us, what would it look like?

_____
_____
_____
_____
_____
_____
_____
_____
_____
_____
_____
_____
_____

RESPONSE

_____
_____
_____
_____
_____

If you could plan a surprise day for us, what would it look like?

_____
_____
_____

_____
_____
_____
_____
_____
_____
_____
_____
_____
_____

RESPONSE

_____
_____
_____
_____
_____

What's something quirky about us as a couple that you love?

_____
_____
_____

_____
_____
_____
_____
_____
_____
_____
_____
_____
_____
_____

RESPONSE

_____
_____
_____
_____
_____

What's something quirky about us as a couple that you love?

_____

_____

_____

_____

_____

_____

_____

_____

_____

_____

_____

_____

_____

RESPONSE

_____

_____

_____

_____

_____

"A strong relationship requires choosing to love each other, even on the days you struggle to like each other."

- Anonymous -

CHAPTER 6

Challenges
and growth

What's a challenge we've faced that made us stronger?

_____
_____
_____
_____
_____
_____
_____
_____
_____
_____
_____
_____
_____

RESPONSE

_____
_____
_____
_____
_____
_____

What's a challenge we've faced that made us stronger?

_____

_____

_____

_____

_____

_____

_____

_____

_____

_____

_____

_____

_____

RESPONSE

_____

_____

_____

_____

_____

How do you think we handle disagreements as a couple?

_____
_____
_____
_____
_____
_____
_____
_____
_____
_____
_____
_____
_____

RESPONSE

_____
_____
_____
_____
_____
_____

How do you think we handle disagreements as a couple?

RESPONSE

What's one thing you'd like us to work on as a team?

_____
_____
_____
_____
_____
_____
_____
_____
_____
_____
_____
_____

RESPONSE

_____
_____
_____
_____
_____

What's one thing you'd like us to work on as a team?

_____
_____
_____
_____
_____
_____
_____
_____
_____
_____
_____
_____
_____
_____

RESPONSE

_____
_____
_____
_____
_____

How do you cope with stress, and how can I support you through it?

_____
_____
_____

_____
_____
_____
_____
_____
_____
_____
_____
_____
_____

RESPONSE

_____
_____
_____
_____
_____

How do you cope with stress, and how can I support you through it?

RESPONSE

What's one way we can handle conflict better in the future?

_____

_____

_____

_____

_____

_____

_____

_____

_____

_____

_____

_____

_____

RESPONSE

_____

_____

_____

_____

What's one way we can handle conflict better in the future?

RESPONSE

What's something you've learned from our toughest moments?

_____

_____

_____

_____

_____

_____

_____

_____

_____

_____

_____

_____

_____

RESPONSE

_____

_____

_____

_____

_____

What's something you've learned from our toughest moments?

_____

_____

_____

_____

_____

_____

_____

_____

_____

_____

_____

_____

RESPONSE

_____

_____

_____

_____

_____

What's something you're proud of in how we've faced challenges together?

_____
_____
_____

_____
_____
_____
_____
_____
_____
_____
_____
_____
_____

RESPONSE

_____
_____
_____
_____
_____

What's something you're proud of in how we've faced challenges together?

_____

_____

_____

_____

_____

_____

_____

_____

_____

_____

_____

_____

_____

RESPONSE

_____

_____

_____

_____

_____

How can we balance time for ourselves with time together better?

_____
_____
_____
_____
_____
_____
_____
_____
_____
_____
_____
_____
_____
_____
_____

RESPONSE

_____
_____
_____
_____
_____

How can we balance time for ourselves with time together better?

RESPONSE

"Intimacy is not purely physical. It's the act of connecting with someone so deeply, you feel like you can see into their soul."

- Anonymous -

Love and
intimacy

When do you feel most connected to me physically?

When do you feel most connected to me physically?

RESPONSE

What's one thing you'd like to explore more in our intimate life?

_____
_____
_____
_____
_____
_____
_____
_____
_____
_____
_____
_____
_____
_____

RESPONSE

_____
_____
_____
_____
_____

What's one thing you'd like to explore more in our intimate life?

RESPONSE

What's one way we can make our intimate moments even more special?

_____
_____
_____
_____
_____
_____
_____
_____
_____
_____
_____
_____
_____
_____
_____

RESPONSE

_____
_____
_____
_____
_____

What's one way we can make our intimate moments even more special?

_____

_____

_____

_____

_____

_____

_____

_____

_____

_____

_____

_____

RESPONSE

_____

_____

_____

_____

What's something I do that makes you feel desired?

_____
_____
_____
_____
_____
_____
_____
_____
_____
_____
_____
_____
_____

RESPONSE

_____
_____
_____
_____
_____
_____

What's something I do that makes you feel desired?

RESPONSE

What's one romantic gesture that means a lot to you?

_____
_____
_____
_____
_____
_____
_____
_____
_____
_____
_____
_____

RESPONSE

_____
_____
_____
_____
_____

What's one romantic gesture that means a lot to you?

_____
_____
_____
_____
_____
_____
_____
_____
_____
_____
_____
_____
_____
_____

RESPONSE

_____
_____
_____
_____
_____
_____

How can we keep our physical connection strong in the future?

_____
_____
_____
_____
_____
_____
_____
_____
_____
_____
_____
_____
_____
_____

_____
_____
_____
_____
_____

How can we keep our physical connection strong in the future?

_____

_____

_____

_____

_____

_____

_____

_____

_____

_____

_____

_____

_____

_____

_____

_____

_____

_____

What does romance mean to you, and how can we incorporate it more into our relationship?

_____
_____
_____
_____
_____
_____
_____
_____
_____
_____
_____
_____
_____

RESPONSE

_____
_____
_____
_____
_____

What does romance mean to you & how can we incorporate it more into our relationship?

_____
_____
_____
_____
_____
_____
_____
_____
_____
_____
_____
_____
_____

RESPONSE

_____
_____
_____
_____
_____

What's your idea of a perfect intimate moment together?

RESPONSE

What's your idea of a perfect intimate moment together?

_____

_____

_____

_____

_____

_____

_____

_____

_____

_____

_____

_____

_____

RESPONSE

_____

_____

_____

_____

_____

"The single biggest problem in communication is the illusion that it has taken place."

- George Bernard Shaw -

Finding our
voice together

How do you prefer to communicate when you're feeling stressed?

_____
_____
_____
_____
_____
_____
_____
_____
_____
_____
_____
_____
_____
_____

RESPONSE

_____
_____
_____
_____
_____

How do you prefer to communicate when you're feeling stressed?

_____
_____
_____
_____
_____
_____
_____
_____
_____
_____
_____
_____
_____

RESPONSE

_____
_____
_____
_____
_____

What's something I could do to be a better listener?

_____
_____
_____
_____
_____
_____
_____
_____
_____
_____
_____
_____
_____
_____

RESPONSE

_____
_____
_____
_____
_____

What's something I could do to be a better listener?

RESPONSE

How can we make sure we stay open and honest in our conversations?

_____
_____
_____
_____
_____
_____
_____
_____
_____
_____
_____
_____
_____
_____

RESPONSE

_____
_____
_____
_____
_____
_____

How can we make sure we stay open and honest in our conversations?

RESPONSE

What's one thing I do that makes you feel heard and understood?

_____
_____
_____
_____
_____
_____
_____
_____
_____
_____
_____
_____
_____
_____

RESPONSE

_____
_____
_____
_____
_____

What's one thing I do that makes you feel heard and understood?

_____

_____

_____

_____

_____

_____

_____

_____

_____

_____

_____

_____

RESPONSE

_____

_____

_____

_____

How can we improve our communication when we disagree?

_____
_____
_____
_____
_____
_____
_____
_____
_____
_____
_____
_____

RESPONSE

_____
_____
_____
_____
_____

How can we improve our communication when we disagree?

_____
_____
_____
_____
_____
_____
_____
_____
_____
_____
_____
_____
_____
_____

RESPONSE

_____
_____
_____
_____
_____

What's one way I can make you feel more comfortable expressing your thoughts?

_____
_____
_____
_____
_____
_____
_____
_____
_____
_____
_____
_____
_____
_____

RESPONSE

_____
_____
_____
_____
_____

What's one way I can make you feel more comfortable expressing your thoughts?

RESPONSE

What's something we could start doing to make our conversations more meaningful?

_____
_____
_____
_____
_____
_____
_____
_____
_____
_____
_____
_____
_____
_____

RESPONSE

_____
_____
_____
_____
_____

What's something we could start doing to make our conversations more meaningful?

RESPONSE

What's one thing we could start doing to make our communication more open?

_____
_____
_____
_____
_____
_____
_____
_____
_____
_____
_____
_____
_____

RESPONSE

_____
_____
_____
_____
_____

What's one thing we could start doing to make our communication more open?

_____

_____

_____

_____

_____

_____

_____

_____

_____

_____

_____

_____

_____

RESPONSE

_____

_____

_____

_____

_____

"The more I see you,
the more I find myself."

- Anonymous -

Seeing you,
seeing us

What's something you admire about me that you've never told me?

_____
_____
_____
_____
_____
_____
_____
_____
_____
_____
_____
_____
_____
_____

RESPONSE

_____
_____
_____
_____
_____

What's something you admire about me that you've never told me?

_____

_____

_____

_____

_____

_____

_____

_____

_____

_____

_____

_____

_____

RESPONSE

_____

_____

_____

_____

_____

What's your favorite memory of us?

_____
_____
_____
_____
_____
_____
_____
_____
_____
_____
_____
_____
_____
_____

RESPONSE

_____
_____
_____
_____
_____

What's your favorite memory of us?

_____
_____
_____

_____
_____
_____
_____
_____
_____
_____
_____
_____
_____

RESPONSE

_____
_____
_____
_____
_____

How do you think I've grown since we first met?

_____

_____

_____

_____

_____

_____

_____

_____

_____

_____

_____

_____

_____

RESPONSE

_____

_____

_____

_____

_____

How do you think I've grown since we first met?

_____

_____

_____

_____

_____

_____

_____

_____

_____

_____

_____

_____

RESPONSE

_____

_____

_____

_____

_____

What's one thing you love about our relationship that's unique to us?

_____
_____
_____

_____
_____
_____
_____
_____
_____
_____
_____
_____
_____
_____

RESPONSE

_____
_____
_____
_____
_____

What's one thing you love about our relationship that's unique to us?

RESPONSE

How do you think we bring out the best in each other?

_____
_____
_____
_____
_____
_____
_____
_____
_____
_____
_____
_____

RESPONSE

_____
_____
_____
_____
_____

How do you think we bring out the best in each other?

RESPONSE

What's one thing I do that makes you feel proud of me?

_____
_____
_____
_____
_____
_____
_____
_____
_____
_____
_____
_____
_____

RESPONSE

_____
_____
_____
_____
_____

What's one thing I do that makes you feel proud of me?

RESPONSE

How do you think we balance each other out?

_____
_____
_____
_____
_____
_____
_____
_____
_____
_____
_____
_____
_____
_____

RESPONSE

_____
_____
_____
_____
_____

How do you think we balance each other out?

RESPONSE

What's a small gesture I've made that meant a lot to you?

_____
_____
_____
_____
_____
_____
_____
_____
_____
_____
_____
_____

RESPONSE

_____
_____
_____
_____
_____

What's a small gesture I've made that meant a lot to you?

_____
_____
_____
_____
_____
_____
_____
_____
_____
_____
_____
_____
_____

RESPONSE

_____
_____
_____
_____
_____

"The best is yet to come."

- Frank Sinatra -

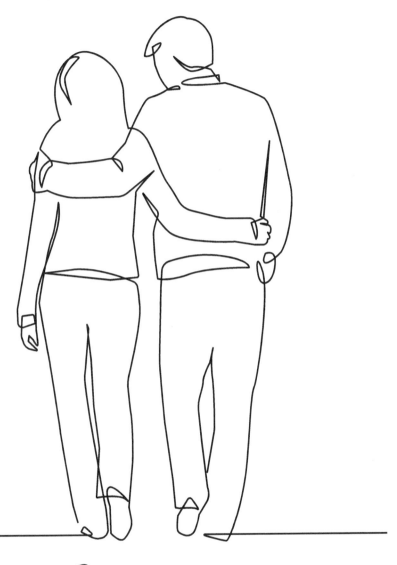

CHAPTER 10

Growing
together

What's a dream or goal we should work toward together?

_____
_____
_____
_____
_____
_____
_____
_____
_____
_____
_____

RESPONSE

_____
_____
_____
_____
_____

What's a dream or goal we should work toward together?

RESPONSE

How do you see our life evolving in the next few years?

_____
_____
_____
_____
_____
_____
_____
_____
_____
_____
_____
_____

RESPONSE

_____
_____
_____
_____
_____

How do you see our life evolving in the next few years?

_____
_____
_____
_____
_____
_____
_____
_____
_____
_____
_____
_____

RESPONSE

_____
_____
_____
_____
_____

What's one adventure you hope we'll take together soon?

_____
_____
_____
_____
_____
_____
_____
_____
_____
_____
_____
_____

RESPONSE

_____
_____
_____
_____
_____

What's one adventure you hope we'll take together soon?

_____

_____

_____

_____

_____

_____

_____

_____

_____

_____

_____

_____

_____

RESPONSE

_____

_____

_____

_____

_____

What's one way we can continue to grow together?

_____
_____
_____
_____
_____
_____
_____
_____
_____
_____
_____
_____
_____

RESPONSE

_____
_____
_____
_____
_____

What's one way we can continue to grow together?

RESPONSE

What's a new tradition we could start this year?

_____
_____
_____
_____
_____
_____
_____
_____
_____
_____
_____
_____
_____
_____

RESPONSE

_____
_____
_____
_____
_____

What's a new tradition we could start this year?

RESPONSE

How can we make time for more fun and spontaneity in our lives?

RESPONSE

How can we make time for more fun and spontaneity in our lives?

RESPONSE

What's a promise you want to make for our future together?

_____
_____
_____
_____
_____
_____
_____
_____
_____
_____
_____
_____
_____
_____

RESPONSE

_____
_____
_____
_____
_____

What's a promise you want to make for our future together?

RESPONSE

What's something that gives you hope for our future?

_____
_____
_____
_____
_____
_____
_____
_____
_____
_____
_____
_____
_____
_____

RESPONSE

_____
_____
_____
_____
_____
_____

What's something that gives you hope for our future?

About the Author:

Emma Grace Harper is a passionate writer and relationship advocate dedicated to helping couples build deeper, more meaningful connections. With a love for journaling, Emma creates guided journals that inspire honest conversations, self-reflection, and intimacy. Her latest book, "Closer Than Ever – A Couples Back & Forth Journal," is designed to encourage couples to share their thoughts, dreams and everyday moments in a unique, engaging way. Emma believes that strong relationships are built one page - and one heartfelt exchange - at a time.

When not writing, she enjoys spending time with family, exploring nature, and delving into historical biographies.

Emma would be incredibly grateful if you could help others discover her books on Amazon by leaving a review. Your feedback not only supports her work but also helps others find and enjoy her journals. Thank you for your support!

Dear Reader,

The journey we take together, the shared laughter, and the moments of vulnerability - each exchange weaves together a beautiful, shared story. ***Closer Than Ever – A Back & Forth Journal for Couples*** is crafted to help you and your partner connect on a deeper level. With thoughtful prompts and engaging questions, this journal encourages you both to reflect, laugh, and dream, creating a space to document the unique bond you share.

Gifting this journal to your partner or using it together is an invitation to slow down, to listen, and to uncover new layers of understanding. In our fast-paced world, the beauty of true connection can sometimes be overlooked. This journal transforms your reflections and responses into a meaningful keepsake, capturing the journey of your relationship, one page at a time.

Check out my other Bonded By Stories journals, each designed to help loved ones connect with one another:

- Mom, Tell Me Your Story

- Dad, Tell Me Your Story

- Grandma, Tell Me Your Story

- Grandpa, Tell Me Your Story

To explore digital journaling options and my other journals, please visit **www.bondedbystories.com** or **scan the QR code** below.

With love,
Emma Grace Harper

Made in United States
Troutdale, OR
12/15/2024

26536889R00106